In-Laws and All

A SURVIVAL GUIDE

Bracha Loren, Psy.D, LMFT

LUMINARE PRESS

WWW.LUMINAREPRESS.COM

In-Laws and All
Copyright © 2020 by Bracha Loren

Printed in the United States of America

Cover Design by Claire Flint Last

Luminare Press
442 Charnelton St.
Eugene, OR 97401
www.luminarepress.com

LCCN: 2020902171
ISBN: 978-1-64388-294-9

Dedicated with love to my grandchildren.

TABLE OF CONTENTS

Preface vii

Foreword xi

In-Laws 1

Inspiration 3

Navigating the Road 7

Silence is Golden 11

What's In A Name? 17

The Right Partner 23

Bringing It Home 29

Family for Life 33

Open Your Heart 35

Double Standard 39

Stand Up for What's Right 43

No Judgment 47

Money is Not Everything 49

Culture Clash 53

Boundaries 65

Is It Never Too Late? 75

Attitude is Everything 81

In the Bible 87

For Grandparents 97

Len 101

Ingredients for a Fruitful In-Law Relationship 105

End Note 107

Preface

Many years ago, as a young woman approaching my wedding day, my mother told me: "You can't choose your family or your husband's family. But you can choose your friends. So make friends with the family." At the time this was said to me, my focus was on other things - being in love, marriage, plans for the future. I didn't understand the significance or the complexity of what my mother was telling me. Nor did it feel relevant in the moment.

Years later, when I became a relationship specialist, I had the privilege of meeting countless individuals whose sole purpose in our discourse was to improve their relationships and all their nuances. Many individuals were working with me on developing their self-esteem, becoming more assertive in the hopes of presenting themselves in a positive fashion to the world, and improving their connections, in their social milieu, as well as their professional life.

The mainstay of my work, though, has been familial relationships specifically, both with traditionally married and uniquely committed couples. All were striving to remove the obstacles and stumbling blocks that kept them from enjoying smoother unions. The heart of most meetings was to improve the level of communication that would lead to more open and rewarding relationships so that there would be stronger cohesion.

And yet, the relationships that have always stood out to me as particularly special were those between in-laws. Perhaps because of my personal experiences with my in-laws, or perhaps as a result of the issues raised by the individuals I have worked with. Regardless, in-law relationships have become a focus of my practice and I have witnessed countless rewarding resolutions between my patients and their in-laws. And while the focus was initially geared toward the relationship with the in-laws, it inevitably involved the entire family.

"If there were only relationship manuals!" patients would plead time and again. Indeed, when we buy a car we rely on its manual to guide us in operating it, but when it comes to human beings, this is not possible. Each of us is unique. Human beings have individual thoughts, feelings, and different character traits. Since we come from a variety of backgrounds that vary in their circumstances, we react to the world in our own unique manner, from our own perspective. As our experiences differ, our levels of tolerance, values, habits and needs are dissimilar, as well.

Because individuals vary so much, no relationship is like another. As such, each "case" needs to be examined on its own merit; the process of the work must be customized to fit the specific individuals, for it is not possible to find a one-size-fits-all for the perfect, or close to perfect, relationship. Working

Bracha Loren, Psy.D, LMFT

with a specific family is a most delicate process since it demands laser-like attention, and the intention of participants needs to be genuine. When I work with a family that has a new member joining, then the challenge of making the relationship work is even greater.

As with most things in life, an idea starts as a seed. Thirty years ago, I was driving my son's 13-year old friend home from a birthday party. I was telling him a story from my childhood and my son's best friend said to me, "Bracha, with your interesting life, and all the life lessons you've learned, you should write a book." I promised him that as soon as I had something to say that could be helpful to others, or at least interesting and entertaining, I would do just that.

This 13-year-old boy's words never left me, and over the years the idea of sharing my experiences and thoughts on paper would often cross my mind. But I believed that the written word had to carry a meaning not only for me, but for others as well.

Foreword

I met my mother-in-law in January, 1999. It was the same night that I had my first date with her daughter and my now wife, Talia. We were in medical school and on the night of our date, Talia casually informed me that her mother was in town for a few days and asked if I would like to meet her.

Even though it's been twenty years, I remember meeting Bracha Loren for the first time like it was yesterday. We hit it off instantly. She eschewed the typical questions that one would ask of a potential suitor for a daughter, in favor of asking my opinions about religion and politics, the very topics traditionally considered to be off limits in this type of situation! After an hour of spirited discussion we said our goodbyes, but I knew then and there that I had just met someone who would play a prominent role in my life.

Over the years our friendship has grown beyond the typical mother-in-law/son-in-law dynamic. She has become a close friend and confidant. Once during residency in New York I mentioned having a stuffy nose and cough. The next day I received an overnight Fed-Ex delivery from California of frozen home-made soup sealed in individual serve Zip-lock bags.

When it came time to choose a place to settle and raise a family, she travelled to Oregon to scout the area and give us her seal of approval with a promise to fly up and visit regularly (which she has kept without fail). When we experienced a health crisis in the family and needed a helping hand, she arrived ready to do whatever was needed to carry the family through a difficult time.

I often use the words "zest for life" to describe Bracha to others. She's a wonderfully spontaneous person who takes every opportunity to stop and smell the roses. She hums when doing dishes; she dances if she hears music.

Most importantly, she has always treated me more like a son than a son-in-law. The lessons she provides in this book are not just the teachings of a licensed therapist, they are the wise words of a matriarch who has succeeded in building strong relationships with her family, friends, colleagues and, of course, her in-laws.

Enjoy the book!

Gregory Schwartz

In-Laws

The topic of "in-laws" needs to be approached with a great deal of sensitivity and care, as it has proven at times to have the power to make or break a relationship. It can be unpredictable, as it may start out as a very positive relationship and then unexpectedly turn into one of friction. By and large, the reason for this is the result of the people involved having different backgrounds and values, temperaments and levels of tolerance. If one has an argument, for instance, with one's child or a sibling, it can usually be resolved without leaving any remnant of resentment. But as close as one may be to his or her in-laws, with the slightest disagreement the dynamics can change; they are not the family of origin. So the approach to the relationship requires more sensitivity and more consideration to avoid a conflict.

I have worked with many willing individuals and the results have been mostly successful. Of course, I have implemented my education and professional expertise in the process - but have also used the lessons learned from my own life experiences. No one is perfect, and the changes and growth that have shaped me, have been a guiding light in my work.

In my first marriage, my husband and I were blessed with 4 children. While the marriage ultimately ended in divorce after 13 years, I look back with appreciation that when there were conflicts, of which there were plenty, between my in-laws and myself, my ex-husband always supported me. The negative relationship that I experienced with them helped to shape my future dealings with my own children's spouses.

I fell in love again and married my second husband. Unfortunately, he passed away 23 years later when his heart tragically failed. My dear parents had passed away two years earlier, my mother first and then my father the following year. Experiencing the death of three loved ones in such a short period of time gave me a special appreciation for life. I am very grateful for my adult children and the nine grandchildren they have blessed me with, all of whom have added tremendous flavor and vitality to my life. With this appreciation has come the desire to help others look at life through a brighter lens and welcome the positive aspects that life can offer.

Inspiration

Several years ago, I gave a talk on relationships to a gathering of 25 women. When the subject of in-laws came up, it created such sparks; everyone was talking over one another. They all had something to say about a daughter-in-law or a son-in-law and their parents. When I suggested that perhaps mothers-in-law should also take into account what they do or do not do, silence filled the room. Driving home that day, I reflected on how each of the women I had just met had their own story to tell - struggles and triumphs. Whatever the relationship between adult child and parents, it will quite often be affected by a new partner coming into the family.

While most of my patients have sought my guidance due to negative experiences with their in-laws, I also have had the pleasure of encountering some beautiful and inspiring in-law relationships.

Sarah

It was a sunny California day when I stumbled upon a gallery, where an artist was working on a portrait of a beautiful woman that was commissioned by her daughter-in-law, Sarah. I was fascinated by the apparent love and admiration Sarah felt for her husband's mother. It is not something that one hears about too often. It inspired me. It also caused flash-backs of my own dark experiences as a daughter-in-law during my first marriage, when I was new to this country, far from my own family. Those were days of sadness and disappointment and it made me appreciate Sarah's situation even more.

Meeting Sarah's mother-in-law was my next objective. I asked the artist to introduce us and we ended up having tea together. I was delighted to find myself sitting across from Eva, a distinguished looking, gentle, older woman, elegantly dressed in a stylish grey suit, a yellow chapeau with grey feather well situated on her head, and white gloves in one hand. She looked as if she had just stepped out of a 1920's fashion magazine. "Is this for real?" I wondered.

She wore an inviting smile and had a glimmer in her eye. After the traditional greetings between strangers, Eva thanked me for inviting her to tea, saying, "Don't mind my appearance, dear. I love dressing up and I don't get out that often anymore." Then she told me, "The portrait is done and it is utterly to my liking. Sarah was wonderful to do this for me."

When I asked Eva the secret to the extraordinary relationship with her daughter-in-law, her response was, "mutual love and respect." These ideas were not new to me but seeing their application in the real world was what impressed me so. Millions of thoughts ran through my mind on that day, and a light went on in my head, "IN-LAWS!" I knew the seed had sprouted - my book had just begun.

Through examples and vignettes that I will share with you, the reader, I will convey the conclusions that I have reached during a lifetime of experience, with the hope that you will draw your own conclusions that will help you navigate through life in the direction of the harmony you deserve.

Navigating the Road

A husband and wife are driving along the freeway.

The scenery is lovely—rolling green hills and cows grazing in a distant pasture— an idyllic image.

They are arguing, throwing insults at each other.

Looking at the cows,

Husband: "Family of yours?"

Wife: "Yes. My in-laws!"

—Unknown

As we navigate through life and our relationships, finding the balance between staying true to ourselves while co-existing peacefully with others remains a life-long challenge. Learning to understand the nuances of these relationships will allow us to thrive more harmoniously and effectively.

Familial relationships are complicated even among individuals who have been together for a lifetime, let alone additional new "arrivals." Those newly joining a family will undoubtedly experience interactions that are different from the ones they grew up with. In such situations, it is easy to be judgmental and disapproving of one another. What may seem "different" to a newcomer may be natural to their partner and the partner's family. This is where the elements of acceptance and staying within one's own boundaries enter, to "protect" both sides from clashing. It is the same with parents: when they notice interactions between the new couple that they may not approve of, they too need to be cognizant of their boundaries and respectfully accept the new reality. It needs to be clear to all parties that whatever does not seem "right" to them, still works for others and is not subject to judgment. The new couple, comprised of two distinct individuals, creates a new dynamic, a new style, a new standard that will be unique to them. The sooner it is understood and accepted, the sooner harmony will lodge within the family.

Some parents may feel threatened when their child chooses a mate. Is it the fear of loss? Is it the fear of being replaced? Is it the fear of not being needed? Is it the fear of becoming irrelevant? Is it the fear of no longer being special? Is it the reluctance to share or give up control, to stop being the "only ones?" Could it be unfulfilled expectations? Of course, it can be any or all of the above.

Thus begins the in-law challenge.

"In-Laws" is a universally loaded subject that has supplied a great deal of material even for comedians. However, we all know that it is not funny for those involved in a difficult relationship. The in-law relationship, stereotypically depicted in a negative light, is perhaps the most complex relationship.

Once two people decide to tie the knot, they enter a relationship with the entire family of their partner. The newlyweds hope to be embraced lovingly by the new families and to be accepted by them unconditionally, and the new family wishes for the same. This new alliance in one's life can present as an adventure, a struggle, a problem, or non-issue, depending on which side of the fence you are on or whom you are facing.

Consequently, the scenario can be either wonderful or awful. If it is good, all involved are blessed. If it's lukewarm, once we dig a little we may be met with an overflowing Pandora's Box. A fractured in-law relationship can be quite painful and have negative repercussions on the entire family unit. Yet, this need not be the case. Being open-minded to others' ways of thinking, personalities, and motivations will help these new relationships start on the right foot.

Regardless of the current relationship, if the in-law relationship you are in feels stormy, you are not necessarily up a creek without a paddle. As long as all parties are willing, these relationships can often be fixed by setting aside emotions and applying reason.

Silence is Golden

As hard as it may be, there are times when it is advisable to adhere to the expression "silence is golden." The idea is non-action. The silence discussed here is an active silence. What does that mean? A great deal can be said in response to negative, insulting, upsetting, and degrading remarks; put-downs, if you will. By not reacting we are not losing. Rather, we are demonstrating that we are in control of ourselves and our environment. There is no need to fear being looked at as meek, for the silence here is not the silence of, "I have nothing to say," it is silence by choice, a preferred silence. When we feel the blood rise, when we are emotionally charged, that is precisely the time that we are being tested. It is just when we wish to spill it all out, say it all out of anger or frustration, we must WAIT!

This is the time to determine whether being right is more important than achieving a goal, the time when self-control is put to the test. By choosing to remain silent, we have conquered the impulse to react emotionally and recklessly. We may owe a response but the response will come when we are ready to state it unemotionally and unequivocally. However, let it not be misunderstood; remaining silent is not an act of ignoring the situation or being cold and dismissive. It is simply a way of gathering our thoughts and emotions and then reacting in a thoughtful and rational way when we are ready to confront the situation. Goals may be different, depending on the individual and the circumstances, but in most cases, the goal is for peaceful coexistence and harmony.

My father tried hard to teach me not to "shoot from the hip." Though it took years to learn to stick to silence, it proved itself to be beneficial. My mother, being faithful to the same principle, used to say in her own style, "the tongue has no bones." It is easy for many of us to spontaneously say whatever is on our minds, whenever we feel like it; but how easy is it to take our words back? My mother insisted that one rarely regrets that which has not been said.

Not reacting to certain nuances or statements can go down as a victory; a victory over temper, over thoughtlessness. These can only be destructive in the long run. And with the full cooperation of both partners, the relationship with the rest of the family will become manageable, even gratifying, to all involved.

That being said, this does not mean to put the burden of creating harmony on the newcomer to the family. All involved carry the same responsibility. This means the older in-laws and the rest of the receiving family as well.

In many instances, although there is tension between a mother-in-law and daughter-in-law, the question of whether or not it is worth confronting comes up. I am often asked, "Should I say something, or let it go?" "What do I do when she repeatedly says or does irritating things?" "Is it worth a confrontation?" or "I become so anxious before she comes to visit us because of her behavior."

I propose setting aside your emotions before the visit and envisioning the scenario in your mind. Imagine what will bother you and imagine your reaction. Think about what is most important and what you are trying to accomplish. Weigh whether you want a peaceful visit or to show how frustrated you are. Next, based on your answers to these questions, think about how you *should* react. Not how you *feel*. Keep your goal in mind. If peace and harmony are your ultimate goals, then you must remind yourself that "her" behaviors are probably not a personal reflection unto you, and smile your way through the next few days, realizing that you cannot change another person's nature. Imagine the entire scenario playing out in a peaceful way - this will surely decrease your anxiety about it.

If you have decided that there is a larger issue that you think will be fixed by approaching the other party, but will lead to a greater conflict, you must decide if you are willing to deal with the consequences. The power of words needs to be taken into consideration, for whatever is said cannot be taken back. Thinking ahead with patience is priceless.

MOTHER-IN-LAW BRIDGE

During my last visit in Odessa, Ukraine, I discovered the Mother-In-Law Bridge, свекруха моста. Built in 1968, it is a narrow pedestrian bridge that connects two roads. It was commissioned by the Soviet politician, Mikhail Sinista, who, according to tradition, loved his mother-in-law's pancakes so much that he needed to shorten the way from his house to hers. Another tale connected to the bridge is that when strong winds strike, the structure is known to shake violently, just as a mother-in-law's tongue might. I was very moved by the symbolism of this bridge and what it says about the possibilities of the mother-in-law/son-in-law relationship: A bridge between two cultures, a stronghold of the two families, a direct path between one generation and the next. However, while the bridge is built of concrete and can eventually wear down and break, so too can the mother-in-law/son-in-law relationship, if it is not taken care of and repaired when needing fixing.

While writing this book, I often found myself humming to myself the song "Mother-In-Law," by Ernie K-Doe, which was a number-one hit in 1961. The lyrics describe "Mother-In-Law" as "The worst person I know," and the song depicts the stereotype of a mother-in-law disapproving of the man her daughter chooses to marry. The irony of this song is that Ernie K-Doe had such a close and amicable relationship with his own mother-in-law that, according to his wishes, he was buried next to her!

What's In A Name?

"Oh, I sure am glad to see you, Grandma," the little boy said to his mother's mother. "Now Daddy will do the trick he promised."

The grandmother was curious, "What trick is that?" she asked.

"He told Mommy that he'd climb the walls next time you came to visit," answered the boy.

—UNKNOWN

I love to dance the tango, and I can vouch that it really does take two to tango. Two willing, considerate, respectful and non-judgmental parties, each aware of their own boundaries, have a better chance of communicating successfully on the dance floor and elsewhere.

When two individuals marry, what follows is a potpourri of in-laws on the dance floor: two sets of parents and siblings, and the newlyweds, who have now become their own family unit. Each of the newlyweds will be considered a new addition to a family that has already established certain values, hierarchies and rules of their own.

For a newcomer to fit in and impact positively, the newcomer needs to feel valued and important, not only in the eyes of their partner but by the whole family. At the same time, both the newcomer and the other family members have to accept one another for who they are. Some people are warmer than others, some cooler. Some may be more open and some reticent. Whatever the qualities, they need to be accepted and respected. There is no room for either one to expect the other to change or become different.

This principle was taught to me on my wedding day by my mother. Before I got married the first time, I had the most wonderful relationship with my soon-to-be mother-in-law. When I first met her she reminded me of Lucille Ball. She was just as pretty, sounded like her, and immediate warm feelings toward my future mother-in-law arose in me. At times, I even called her "Lucy" and she loved it, so she would say.

So when shortly after the wedding ceremony, on our way to the reception area, with my mother on one side of me and my mother-in-law on the other, the latter turned to me and sternly told me, "From now on you will call me MOM." I was stunned and at a loss for words. To me, it seemed beyond the pale to make such a request, especially in my mother's presence. After having only experienced positive feelings towards my now mother-in-law until this point, this statement sounded more like a demand than a warm and loving request. I was completely flummoxed.

It was my mother, pinching my arm hard to keep me from reacting, who answered for me, "Of course she will call you Mom." My mother's reaction was very surprising to me. I wanted to preserve her status as "Mom," but she did not mind at all. Later, she told me that she was in fact overjoyed that I would now have two mothers who would love me unconditionally, and that I should respect the rules of my new family. She agreed that although what was said could have been stated with warmth and affection, my mother-in-law's method of expression should not be the take-away from this; it was important for me to value being considered as close as a daughter to my mother-in-law. And even though my mother and I did not know then how this closeness would turn on me, at the time, pleasing my mother-in-law by calling her "Mom" was something that I was happy to do.

While most of us believe that it is best for a bride to be accepted with open arms by her mother-in-law, there are times when a parent of a newlywed is not happy that the parents-in-law welcome their child so openly. As odd as this may seem, it is most often a result of insecurity and defensiveness. I am reminded of a case where a mother wanted to have a monopoly over her own daughter. When the mother found a card sent to her daughter by her mother-in-law, welcoming her to the family and signed, "Mother," she became upset and resentful of the mother-in-law. This instilled similar ill feelings in the daughter. Empathizing with her mother, the daughter told her mother-in-law, "I have only one mother."

That incident planted a bad seed in her relationship with her husband's mother, and many conflicts ensued. All parties shared feelings of rejection, and the husband/son was torn between the two women he loved most, his mother and his wife. In order to resolve this effectively, it was important for the bride to identify the core issue, which was that she was feeling protective of her mother. The bride realized that her loyalty to her mother was not threatened by being accepted by her mother-in-law, as a daughter. Her mother, too, was helped to overcome her initial feelings of fear based on the mistaken assumption that she was losing her daughter. She learned to appreciate her daughter's full acceptance by the new family, and gave up the distorted thinking that someone else was trying to take over. Thankfully, none of the family members were left with any trace of bitterness or resentment.

This example carries a message of encouragement for all parents to respectfully accept their children's partners' families, and the relationship that their children will have with their new in-laws. It is of the essence that parents realize that though their "child" is no one else's but their own, the in-laws do play a significant role in the life of their "child" that cannot be ignored.

When my children were still quite young, I made a conscious decision that when they grew up and married, I would love their partners as my own children, treat them equally well, and accept and respect their families. Because I respect my children and their choices, it has been easy to do. Whomever my children brought home became instant family, as did the families of their beloved. This has helped my children to live harmoniously with their spouses. Based on my own and others' experiences, I have learned that whatever the relationship between adult child and parents, it will be affected by whether or not the parents accept the new partner coming into the family. If they choose to accept the new spouse unconditionally, the relationship between parents and child will be positive. But if they reject the new family member, the relationship is bound to suffer. And who do you suppose benefits the most from this attitude of acceptance? The grandchildren!

Special credit is due to my mother who taught me that a parent should not interfere in the relationship between their adult child and their in-laws. Sometimes, in an effort to maintain exclusivity, one set of parents may engage in ill speaking about their children's in-laws. That will create tension and distance between the parents-in-law, as well as between parents and their children, who will resent the negativity of their parents towards the "new" family. Further, if their child already has negative feelings toward their in-laws, the situation worsens and the parents' interference can cause a conflict that puts harmony in real danger. The wise person will not surrender to such temptation, thus avoiding any unnecessary conflicts.

Bracha Loren, Psy.D, LMFT

The Right Partner

In-law relationships can be complex even without any outside interference. What is it that makes the relationships with in-laws so different from other relationships we have in our lives? Why are there so often complications?

We can assume that most parents of all cultures invest a great deal of love and effort in raising their children. They would likely enjoy seeing their sons and daughters meet the "right" partners and move on to build a happy life with them. No parent would plan to be a rejecting, disrespecting, unaccepting or unloving in-law.

As children grow up, parents' expectations of them become clearer, both to themselves and their children. Some may have a clear idea of who they think their child will marry and in some cultures parents even choose the child's future partner. But most parents in Western society are faced with a fait accompli. Though it may not be the person the parents had hoped for, their child has decided on a mate with whom they wish to build a home. The age-old questions such as, "Is this partner good enough for my child?" "Will my child be taken care of?" are not for the parents to answer. The sole decision makers are the newly united couple. The parents, unless asked, will be wise not to interfere.

My first mother-in-law did not expect her son to marry a foreigner! Throughout our marriage, she would remind me that she had introduced her son to a wonderful American nurse, saying, "All the foreign girls catch the best American boys." When a partner comes into a new family, how overwhelming it can be to meet, not only the parents, but the expanded family, siblings, cousins, uncles and aunts, all of whom have certain expectations of the newcomer. How treacherous it can be when the message given to the newcomer is that they are not good enough. The newcomer is in a peculiar position. Do they take a position of, "it's either me or your parents?" Or, does the adult child choose to reject their own parents, in order to make peace with their new spouse? Reaching the proper balance between unmet expectations, as well as dealing and accepting reality, is the challenge.

Often the moment a new partner joins a family, the dynamics change. It is difficult not to project our expectations or behaviors onto others and we must respectfully realize that others' reactions are not always personal. Nevertheless, it would be prudent on the part of parents-in-law to remember how it was for them when they started, new and inexperienced, and how long it took for them to feel unconditionally accepted by their partners' parents.

There was a telling commercial advertising spices on television, where a daughter-in-law asked her mother-in-law, "Why is it that my husband does not stop praising your cooking. He always says, "My mother's food, my mother's food!" What do you do that I don't?" The wise mother-in-law responded, "I will teach you that it isn't what you cook, it's what you put into it." She then proceeded to open a large cupboard full of spices, offering them, her secrets, to her daughter-in-law.

Though this is a commercial, it is a wonderful lesson of what should happen, with both parties accepting each other unconditionally. It is an ideal example of a daughter-in-law who feels safe enough to approach her mother-in-law and admit that she needs help.

Acceptance allows freedom and safety in the relationship. She is letting her mother-in-law know, in all honesty, and without concern of being judged, that she needs guidance, that she looks up to her and wishes to learn from her. The wise and kind mother-in-law is showing acceptance and willingness to share, to teach, to relinquish control and let her secrets be known, thus contributing to the couple's happiness, and her son's welfare.

No one wants to be labeled "monster in-law." We want to assume that any reasonable father-in-law or mother-in-law would be happy to teach their child's partner how to make their own child happy. Every newcomer into a family, regardless of age, can learn from their partner's parents. Whether it be small details about likes and dislikes, favorite dishes, or any idiosyncrasies. Connecting on this level and sharing past experiences will serve to enhance and strengthen the relationship.

We too often hear of a newcomer feeling rejected, unaccepted, and not included by the parent-in-law. Such feelings can instill insecurities that might make the newcomer feel challenged to outdo their partner's parent. In such cases there is a missed opportunity on both sides to get to know each other and become family. Mutual respect, acceptance and humility, are key ingredients in achieving harmony. When these are present and maintained by both parties, the result is a "win-win" situation.

The following pages are meant to guide the reader in how to successfully overcome these obstacles, and bring peace to the countless relationships within the expanded family.

My mother, *Ima'le*, circa 1938, Palestine

Bringing It Home

This idea is reflected in a story that my mother shared with me about her mother-in-law. My parents, both young and in love, came from similar backgrounds, but my father's mother opposed their union. She would not accept my mother; she did not even show up at my parents' wedding! Her misinformed reasoning was that my mother was not good enough because she would not be able to bear children due to her practice of riding horses. This was an erstwhile myth, an old wives' tale that my grandmother bought into.

My mother, orphaned at a very young age, wished whole-heartedly to "belong" with my father's family. She was even willing to forgive her mother-in-law for boycotting the wedding, but it wasn't to be. My father yearned to build a home with my mother and was looking forward to having a harmonious, fulfilled life with her. He wanted her to be accepted and treated as part of the family. Above all, he wanted his mother to embrace his wife. However, my grandmother would ridicule my mother at any given opportunity, such as my mother's lack of knowledge about cooking, a most valued skill at the time that every wife was expected to master, while at the same time refusing to teach her. As time went on, to the dismay of my grandmother, my mother learned on her own to become a wonderful cook. Grandmother never failed to remind her, "mine is better." Understandably, this attitude did not ignite feelings of love in my mother.

My grandmother did not realize that a willingness to guide her daughter-in-law would not only strengthen their relationship, but it would make her son happy. Instead, she chose to maintain her exclusivity by holding on to her status as head of the family. She fiercely guarded the secrets of her kitchen and continued to mistreat my mother. Her lack of generosity pained my father and resentment toward her brewed in him. With this dark cloud hanging over them, the loving relationship between my father and his mother was bound to deteriorate; from a loving relationship, it turned into one of obligation. My great consolation, though, is that regardless of the difficulties that my parents experienced with my grandmother, my parents shared a life of mutual respect, love and friendship, and in this spirit they raised their three children.

In all fairness, without blaming the older in-laws exclusively, perhaps there was something that my mother could have done to remedy the situation. Being the victim does not necessarily imply that one cannot take initiative. Looking at this situation objectively, if my mother had come to me as a patient, I would have encouraged her to reach out to her mother-in-law in ways beyond the kitchen, such as inviting my grandmother to coffee, going for a walk together, visiting her alone and sitting and talking together. Anything to open the relationship and show that she was not a threat to her. However, we must keep in mind that there is no guarantee when dealing with a person who is not willing to open the door to the relationship.

Neither my mother nor my grandmother realized the implications of the animosity that grew between them. Unfortunately, short-sightedness on both parts, with regard to their children and their grandkids, resulted in paying a high price. A manipulative, non-inclusive person who tries to be "the only one," makes others feel left out in the process. Such a person is liable to lose at a later stage by alienating themselves from others. My grandmother lost greatly. The distance between her and my parents grew wider and wider and the grandchildren (my siblings and I) never got close to her, leaving no winners in either court. No grandparent that I know of would be willing to sacrifice the relationship with their grandchildren, but this is often an unavoidable consequence of a fractured relationship. Thus, maintaining that relationship is good incentive for in-laws to be kind to one another and mindful of their own openness.

Bracha Loren, Psy.D, LMFT

Family for Life

DENISE

Denise is an American woman who married into a family newly arrived from Italy. She worked hard to learn their language, which opened up for her a window into the Italian culture, and facilitated her ability to connect with the family members who did not speak English. Denise was lucky to join a family who embraced her with love and affection, and they were appreciative of her interest in their culture. Her mother-in-law, Sofia, was happy to share her pearls of wisdom with her new daughter-in-law, along with her secrets of the Italian kitchen. The two women remained close and loving for many years, even long after Denise had divorced Sofia's son, which allowed Sofia the good fortune of continuing to enjoy her grandchildren, with Denise's encouragement.

Many years later, when Denise became a mother-in-law, she hoped to have the same type of relationships with her two daughters-in-law. One of them was more open to the inclusive relationship Denise offered, and they enjoyed a close relationship; the other young woman preferred to have a more formal relationship, which Denise accepted. Her ultimate goal was for her sons to be happy, achievable only by offering and maintaining mutual respect and understanding with both new families. The peaceful and harmonious relationships that resulted were greatly appreciated by both her sons.

It was so refreshing as a therapist to see how much insight Denise had in this situation, as she was able to adjust to what made each of her daughters-in-law comfortable, without having either feel as if they didn't share the same bond. Denise realized that different personalities have different needs and being able to accommodate for this allowed both relationships to flourish in their own way.

Open Your Heart

BECKY AND JULIAN

When Becky and Julian's son, Matthew, met Jessica, they believed that she was a wonderful match for him. She was successful, intelligent, and beautiful, and the young couple appeared to be in love. She seemed considerate of and interested in the family and they felt she would be an ideal addition to it. So enamored was Becky, that she would kiddingly declare, "If my son does not propose to her, I will!"

Eventually he did propose. But soon after the lavish wedding, Jessica began to overstep her boundaries by interfering between Matthew and his parents, and began to create intrigues among her sisters-in-law and brothers-in-law. Jessica's compulsion to control and manipulate her new family members was bound to become detrimental to this loving and peaceful family and Matthew began to sense the tension.

After sleepless nights of remorse and worry, Becky and Julian wondered, "Did we put too much pressure on our son to get married?" They decided to put aside all emotions and consider the issue impartially. But of course, this was no easy task and after speaking with their son, asked his permission for Becky to have a "heart to heart" with Jessica. She knew she was taking a risk in doing so, and with her son's approval, Becky invited Jessica for lunch to open the dialogue. It was in no way Becky's intension to hurt her daughter-in-law or make her feel uncomfortable, as she understood that insecurity was at the core of Jessica's behavior. Becky's intention was to delicately approach Jessica to redirect emotions. She used her wisdom and acted as an inclusive mother-in-law by letting Jessica know that she was loved and that she was a welcome addition to the family, thus opening a line of communication between the two women. Jessica had the opportunity to explain herself and they each realized that multiple miscommunications had led them to this point. As a result, the two women became closer and with time developed a lovely friendship. This also strengthened the bond between Becky and Julian with their son. This was a successful intervention that repaired the relationship within the family and freed Matthew and Jessica from the tension that existed in their relationship.

The openness and honesty that Becky employed achieved the objective for there to be harmony in the family, and life became more pleasant for all involved. It also set the precedent of talking honestly about any issues that should arise, allowing Becky and Jessica to move on lovingly.

Double Standard

A mother tells her friend about her children's marriages:

"Oh, my poor son is married to a very demanding wife.

As soon as my son comes home after a tiresome day at work, she expects him to cook and clean and take care of the kids…

My daughter, on the other hand, is married to a wonderful man.

As soon as he is home from work, he cooks and cleans and takes care of the kids."

—Unknown

George and Gary

G&G, as they like to refer to themselves, have lived together since before gay marriage became legal in California. As soon as it did become legal, they got married, with the blessing of both sets of parents. The men have a close relationship with their parents and parents-in-law and with each other's siblings. George is a computer analyst who travels extensively for work, and Gary is a freelance fashion designer. Because he does not have a steady job, Gary is able to travel with George quite a bit.

Early in their marriage, G&G came to me for guidance. George's mother, Estelle, had expressed to Gary her resentment that her son "works so hard and you just go along on vacation." Dumbfounded, Gary did not respond. Until that point, Gary and Estelle had gotten along so well and he was upset with what he felt was an accusation.

Knowing that Gary and Estelle have a very amicable relationship, I advised Gary to speak with Estelle directly, as I saw no need to triangulate George into the situation. Gary suggested coming in to my office with Estelle, should the conversation escalate into a conflict. Although Estelle was not entirely comfortable with the idea of therapy, she complied, and Gary had the opportunity to point out her double standard. He reminded her how pleased she was that her daughter joined her husband on his work related trips.

There was no argument nor any accusation in this dialogue between mother-in-law and son-in-law, just reasonable, sincere communication between adults. Gary explained how hurt he was by Estelle's words, especially because of their close relationship. Realizing Gary was right, George's mother admitted that she did indeed have a double standard; she thanked Gary for being so kind in dealing with her. "He's right, and I realize I have some things to learn about myself, after all," she told me.

Having insight and the willingness to be open enough to admit when one is wrong, is crucial in any successful relationship. Conversely, for the relationship to thrive, individuals must also be willing to accept the apology and move on. Gary and Estelle are a good example of accepting responsibility and reconciliation.

Stand Up for What's Right

DEBORAH AND ALAIN

Both sets of parents were very happy when Deborah and Alain married. As wedding gifts, Deborah's parents gave the couple a condo in the posh part of the city where they were living, and Alain's parents furnished it for them. All in-laws got along beautifully.

A few years later, when Deborah's brother married, Alain believed that his mother-in-law, a widow by then, gave her son more money than she had given to Deborah and him as newlyweds. Alain announced to Deborah that unless her mother were to give them the equal amount of money as the brother received, she was not welcome in their home. Indeed, until her dying day, this mother never again set foot in her daughter's home.

"It was so painful not to have my mom with us on holidays and other family gatherings," lamented Deborah. "But Alain is a stubborn man. We had a high standard of living, which I did not want to change, and

I did not want to become a divorcee." In those days, no matter how bad it was, most women stayed in the marriage. She told me that though her selfless mother knew about Alain's demands, she advised Deborah not to fight with him, and agreed not to visit them in their home.

Deborah and her only daughter did get together at her mother's home, although not too often. Until this day, she rues her decision. "It was a great mistake on my part to agree to Alain's demands. And I can never make up for the hurt and humiliation my mother suffered. It makes my heart ache with regret," Deborah stated.

I met Deborah several years after her mother passed away. Old wounds had reopened when her daughter was planning her wedding, for Deborah had never forgiven herself or her husband for their treatment of her late mother. Deborah relayed to me what transpired during a conversation she and Alain had with their daughter and future son-in-law, before the wedding. The soon-to-be newlyweds were planning to honor the grandparents at their wedding. Her daughter was very disappointed that she never had a close relationship with her grandmother; she could never comprehend why her parents had treated her grandmother in such a shameful way. At that point in the conversation, Deborah turned to Alain with an accusing look, and he said, "You went along with it, and you agreed that there was injustice done to us!"

Their daughter asked for a detailed explanation, at the end of which she asked her father, "How would you feel if Sean treated you how you treated Grandma?" It was at this point that Deborah "decided to talk the whole thing over with a third party."

I suggested to Deborah that though Alain had been the one to outwardly mistreat her mother, she and Alain were "partners in crime," so to speak; Alain needed to realize the gravity of the mistake that had been made and Deborah needed to come to terms with the role that she played. Indeed, it was definitely too late to make amends to her mother, but an apology to their daughter, and sincere expression of regret, needed to come from both of them.

It took Alain a while until he was ready to accept responsibility and admit to his daughter his appalling disrespect towards his mother-in-law and his lack of gratitude for what she had done for him and Deborah financially when they got married. Furthermore, he admitted that for so long he looked forward to the day that he would have a son-in-law, being that they only had one child, and that he would be crushed if he did not have that relationship. Sharing the blame with Alain eased the pain Deborah was feeling and with a heavy heart they both asked forgiveness from their daughter. Alain later told Deborah that what he was most grateful to her mother for was how she accepted him unconditionally even after he had treated her so terribly.

No Judgment

DAVID AND REUBEN

David and Reuben have been partners for 12 years and are lovingly accepted by each other's families. They live in a condo that David bought himself when he graduated from college. It is near David's parents' home, and the couple spends considerable time there, enjoying meals and other gatherings. Reuben says, "I love watching sports on TV with David's father."

When David first moved into his own place, his mother would come over to clean his condo regularly. "You know how men are," she would say. She continued to "straighten up," even after Reuben moved in with him.

Initially, her actions were somewhat surprising to Reuben, who interpreted David's mother's behavior as unusual. But he refrained from commenting and has come to accept that this makes her happy. Their criteria for boundaries are different from others. Reuben says, "We all have our idiosyncrasies, that's hers."

What works for one couple may not work for others and that is precisely why there are no strict rules about behavior. It is unproductive to be judgmental or project one's own standards on others, as people should make their own choices that fit in with their unique situations.

Furthermore, the way in which Reuben handled this situation displays a concept that I feel is very important to comment on. Many couples openly discuss their dissatisfaction with each other's families. While closeness and honesty between partners is ideal, it is essential that one considers whether their comments will be presented in a way that is hurtful for the other partner to hear. It is often difficult to be told how "terrible" or "annoying" one's mother, father, sister, or brother is. We must not forget that this is your partner's family and the family that raised your partner. Consider expressing yourself in a way that is not demeaning or resorting to name calling, which may lead to defensiveness and ultimately derail the original intention of the conversation.

Bracha Loren, Psy.D, LMFT

Money is Not Everything

BELLA AND SIMON

Bella and her husband Aaron, and Simon and his wife Riva, immigrated to the U.S. together from the "Old Country" and kept the friendship going for many years. Each couple had a daughter; the two daughters were as close as were their parents.

Years later, both Bella and Simon lost their spouses. Simon remained in his home and Bella eventually moved in with her daughter and her family. Consequently, Simon and Bella were no longer in close contact. Concerned about their parents growing old and lonely, both Simon's and Bella's daughters planned a dinner to bring their parents together.

It was not long before Simon and Bella began a romantic relationship, to the delight of their daughters. When the old friends got married, the two families became one, as they had been in spirit since the very start. Bella and Simon became step-parents to each other's daughters, whom they had known since their infancy. Bella moved into Simon's home and life seemed perfect.

One year after the wedding, Bella asked Simon to will his house to her to ensure her financial security should he pass away before her. Simon was not pleased with this request; his daughter was to inherit the house. His refusal hurt Bella and the relationship began to change. The once happy atmosphere turned to one of angry silence. Each daughter could not help but notice, especially during festive occasions. Simon shared Bella's request with his daughter and her husband, and they began to wonder if Bella had ulterior motives. Bella claimed that they did not understand her.

It was at this point when the family decided to see me in my office. In order to evaluate the situation, I first spoke to the older couple. As she told me of her fears of "remaining with nothing," Bella began to cry. "I lost one husband," she sobbed, "and I'm scared to be alone again." She added that should she lose Simon, she would be completely dependent on her daughter.

Simon was quiet while his wife poured her heart out. When I turned to him, I saw his eyes were tearing. "What am I going to tell my daughter?" he asked. "My late wife and I willed the house to her years ago." He wished to ensure that Bella would be independent and well taken care of in the event of his death, but he felt lost as to how to face his daughter. On their way

Bracha Loren, Psy.D, LMFT

out of my office they were holding hands for the first time in weeks.

The next meeting at my office took place a few days later with Bella's daughter, as well as Simon's daughter and her husband, Daniel. The latter initially expressed anger towards Bella. "She is not who she used to be," they said. They were disappointed that she would marry Simon for money. Bella's daughter felt embarrassed by her mother's request and about her own limited ability to provide for her mother, should she be left alone. "I'd do anything for my mother, but with my husband not working, it's getting harder and harder." At that point, Simon's daughter began to cry, admitting that she may have been too quick to judge Bella. She told Bella's daughter that after thinking about it honestly, she actually understood "where your mom is coming from." She added, "We love your mom but don't know what to do." Daniel asked if they could all meet again with Bella and Simon there. Seeing that the crisis could end favorably, I told them I thought it was a good idea.

At the next session, the whole family, including Simon and Bella, gathered in my office. Daniel took the lead by respectfully and gently approaching Bella saying, "We love you. Not only are you my mother-in-law now, but you have been like a mother to my wife for many years. We want you to be happy." He then asked Bella what was on her mind.

Bella was honest and explained that ever since "Uncle Aaron" passed away she has felt like a burden to her daughter. Bella did not marry Simon for money. She loved him; they had always been close friends and she knew the kind of man he was. Simon's eyes were tearing as Bella spoke.

Daniel suggested a solution that he and his wife had agreed on beforehand. The house would be given to Bella, should Simon pass away, and willed to Simon's daughter, should Bella pass away. Daniel explained, "I am doing well financially and we just want you and Simon to be happy." Bella's daughter was relieved and grateful for this kindness.

As we all know too well, money has the power to threaten even the most peaceful and loving families. Too often I have seen this break families apart and cause long-lasting animosity that cannot be fixed. Working with this family gave me a new perspective on what can be achieved with gratitude, empathy, openness and generosity.

Culture Clash

Today, we live in a world where many cultures come together, a far cry from the past, when most of the populous were limited to their specific countries. People immigrate to new countries; others take to travel for business, pleasure, education and a plethora of other purposes. People of different cultures inevitably meet, socialize, and quite often end up connecting romantically and marrying. As such, some families accept whomever their son or daughter will choose to marry, regardless of their origins. Others, however, are appalled by such unions.

ABE

"I hate my daughter-in-law," Abe confessed to me. It was his dream that his son, Rick, would someday marry into a family of his own cultural background. It did not occur to him that raising his son in the U.S, a multi-cultural society, would open the possibility that he would choose a partner "outside" of their culture. But that's exactly what happened.

Abe never accepted his daughter-in-law or "her people." As a result, he projected a negative opinion on everything about her, even the way she raised his grandchildren. "Sharon's a horrible person," he decried, "...spending my son's money." Since the day he met her, he could not come to terms with the fact that Sharon was family. He respected neither her nor her requests regarding the grandchildren, and was not mindful of his boundaries. The fact that Rick was happy with his wife did not matter to him. "I told my son not to marry her, and I still let him know how I feel about her."

Abe was seldom invited to see his grandchildren because of his unreasonable and demeaning behavior toward Sharon. When Sharon would ask Abe to refrain from discussing certain topics with or around the kids, he would say, "I don't need to listen to you, they are my grandchildren...If my son had married a woman from our country, she would know how to raise the kids the right way."

Not trusting how Abe would treat Sharon in his absence, and wanting to protect her, Rick has chosen to avoid any possible confrontation by distancing his father from his family when he is not there to watch over. Consequently, Abe felt isolated from his family. "That means I don't get to see the kids much and that hurts." Despite knowing full well why he was kept away from the family at times, Abe refused to change his treatment of his daughter-in-law. He believed his behavior was reasonable and justified. He regretted that, "My grandchildren hardly know me," but remained determined not to give up his principles: "If I don't like her, I'm not going to pretend."

After years of mistreatment by her father-in-law, Sharon was happy that Abe rarely visited. Fortunately, her relationship with her father-in-law, or lack of it, has not affected her relationship with her husband. Abe came over only when Rick was home and she never had to host him on her own. Certainly, the kids, who barely knew him, hardly missed him.

Abe was not able to recognize in himself that his attitude towards Sharon was completely clouded by his prejudice. Realizing that Abe did not actually know Sharon at all, but was purely judging her based on her cultural background, I thought it was time for him to get to know her. I suggested that Sharon and Rick join Abe in his next session, which they agreed to, and I commended Sharon on her willingness and courage to face Abe.

During that session, Rick confronted his father about his "disgusting bigotry." He continued by stating that his children, whom Abe claims to love so much, are partially Sharon's culture and partially his culture. He explained that if Abe wasn't able to accept Sharon and where she comes from, then he was no longer welcome in their home. Rick continued by opening up about the bigotry and intolerance that he had been raised with and how he no longer wished to expose himself or his family to it.

Abe and Sharon both sat speechless, each for a different reason. Sharon was proud of and grateful to her husband; Abe finally realized that there was a lot he did not know and felt embarrassed and humiliated.

The next time I saw Abe was several weeks later. He told me that he and Rick had not had any contact since the last session. Rick told Abe that he would like distance and Abe came to understand and accepted his own part in the deterioration of the relationship. He asked for help in repairing the relationship with Rick and Sharon, recognizing that it would take much time and effort.

Abe was perhaps my most difficult patient to work with but at the end, he surprised me more than any other patient I have ever seen. While I had been trying all along to help him develop insight into his prejudices, the source of his intolerance, he remained resistant and insisted that, "You don't know Sharon. If you did you would know what I'm talking about." It took Rick, his son, who knew him best, to finally reach him. But an event that unexpectedly took place a few months later would be the impetus that would ultimately repair the relationship. Rick needed emergency back surgery and Sharon called Abe telling him that it would give Rick great pleasure to see them together at his bedside. Abe took this gesture as forgiveness from Sharon and accepted her invitation. He continued to help her in her husband's absence and with time, Sharon and Abe have begun to appreciate each other. The last time I saw Abe, Rick was on his way to physical recovery, while the family as a whole was continuing the process of emotional healing.

RAFFI

I am reminded of Raffi, a taxi driver, whom I met in Israel as I was making my way from Tel Aviv to Jerusalem. Upon discovering my background in couple's therapy, Raffi began to open up to me during the long ride. "I just divorced my wife of fifteen years." His was the first divorce in the family. The "badgering" about his mother became unbearable, he explained.

Raffi told me that he and his wife were of different cultural and socio-economic backgrounds. His family, although poor, was warm and welcoming. His wife came from an affluent family, and Raffi always felt that they were distant and cold. Despite their differences, Raffi's mother accepted her daughter-in-law and welcomed her with open arms, always trying to "make her feel at home." According to Raffi, every time they would leave his mother's house, his wife would criticize his mother, referring to her as "primitive," which he found humiliating, not only for his mother, but for him and his siblings. To Raffi, his wife behaved like she was "doing us a favor" by joining his family.

Raffi's mother had raised him and his five siblings with much difficulty. They were very poor growing up, and now Raffi and his siblings support their mother financially in her old age. This act of "taking care" of elderly parents is very much a part of Raffi's culture, but was something entirely foreign to his wife, and she could not accept it. "We have three kids!" she would shout. His wife did not understand the pride that her husband felt in being able to help support his mother. This discord between Raffi and his wife escalated to the point where it affected the children. Hearing what their mother would say about their father's family, they began to feel insecure about who they were.

Raffi was a man in pain and was grateful to be able to open up to a complete stranger. Of course, he could only tell his truth, his side of the story. Painful as it was, one could not make an objective determination without hearing his wife's side of the story as well. But what I did take away from Raffi's story is the importance of understanding the culture that one is entering upon marriage. Culture is not simply the food, clothing and language; those are the external expressions of one's culture. To know another's culture is to understand the family dynamics, the customs and often the cultural obligations. If one is entering a family of a different culture, it is essential to learn as much as possible about that culture, its nuances and expectations, and to evaluate how easy or hard it would be to join that family.

When Raffi and I said goodbye, I thanked him for opening up to me and wished him good luck. His story was on my mind that whole day. I reflected on how much culture and upbringing influence who we are. I wished that I had met Raffi and his ex-wife at the beginning of their relationship, for that is when it is most important to take the time to "learn" a family.

Often, a newcomer, in love, with hopes and dreams, decides to join in, accepting and wishing to be part of the new family, and is accepted in return. However, the deeper cultural nuances take time to become apparent. This is why spending time together and inquiring about the family history is so essential.

MALIN AND EUGENE

Eugene, an American born man, was married to Malin, a first generation American born woman. Their relationship seemed ideal from the outset, but Eugene had a great, hidden resentment toward Malin's parents. He had no complaints about their treatment of him; they were cordial and respectful. His difficulty was accepting them.

Eugene's parents-in-law perceived his behavior as reserved and well-mannered. They did not understand that his lack of engagement with them was actually due to his negative feelings towards them. To me, Eugene would say he had complete dislike for them. He objected to his wife speaking in her mother-tongue when communicating with her parents, even though her parents did not speak English. "Let them learn English," he would say. He insisted that when they have children, her parents should speak with them only in English.

When he expressed the wish that his parents-in-law should go back to the "old country," Malin decided that she'd had enough; she was feeling "caged in by Eugene's limited ability to accept my family," in her words. She wanted her freedom and, above all, wanted to reclaim her parents' honor. After two years of marriage Malin was ready to divorce Eugene. When she told Eugene of her decision, he was completely shocked and distraught. I met the couple at this point, when

Malin told Eugene that the only way to save the marriage was to attend couples-therapy.

Malin had never stood up to Eugene before and that dynamic allowed him to continue to insult and belittle her parents. Though she loved him deeply, she could not continue to endure his behavior. Eugene pleaded with Malin not to divorce him and so Malin gave him an ultimatum: accept and respect her parents, or she would leave.

Time and again we are reminded that acceptance and respect are mandatory ingredients for harmony. Each in-law, the younger as well as the older, must possess these qualities if they wish for unity. In Eugene and Malin's situation, it was the young in-law who did not initially possess the ability to accept and respect his in-laws for who they were.

In many instances, the spouse whose parents are disrespected does stay in the relationship. They will claim it's for the sake of the kids, for economic security, or some other rationalization. But their quiet suffering will breed resentment, though it may be hidden. Malin did stay in the relationship. Not for children or economic reasons, but because she believed that Eugene really did want to change his attitude.

Once Eugene put aside his pride, he was able to admit that it mattered to him what people might say about his in-laws being old-fashioned and how that might reflect on him. In short, Eugene needed to mature and Malin gave him that chance. This of course was a deeper issue than simply his in-laws not speaking English or dressing in a certain way. It was Eugene's own insecurities and prejudice that led to his poor attitude. Admitting his flaws to himself was a great first step in changing his attitude and willingness to commit to Malin and her family. Initially, Eugene did not understand that by insulting Malin's parents, he was not fully accepting of her, which felt to Malin like a form of betrayal.

Mixed-culture marriages do not necessarily mean trouble. I have seen many patients who harmoniously have integrated their partner's culture into their life and gained great pleasure and enrichment from it. Further, problems in mixed-culture-families are not necessarily due to the cultural difference. This is important to recognize in order not to put the blame on culture when the real issues may actually stem from differences in personalities or temperament.

Boundaries

CARLA AND JEFF

Carla and Jeff, of two different cultural backgrounds, were patients of mine for several months when Jeff hesitantly approached the subject of boundaries during a session. He explained that his father-in-law would consistently visit his and Carla's home when they were not there, clearly overstepping his boundaries. Carla defended her father's actions and explained, "He's just checking on the house. He wants to make sure everything is working well in our home." She continued to explain that her father takes great pride in being "so close to us that he tells all his friends how happy we are that he helps in this way."

In reality, though, Jeff was unhappy about this situation, referring to it as "an intrusion." He tried to relay his displeasure to his father-in-law in various polite and indirect ways but his efforts were ignored. Jeff told Carla that he would like to approach her father directly, since tiptoeing around the issue, as Jeff had done in the past, had not been productive. Carla requested that he be respectful and sensitive in his approach.

In the meeting that ensued, Jeff was very careful not to hurt his father-in-law's feelings, while at the same time assertively expressing his wish for the practice to stop. There was no blaming or criticizing. On the contrary, Jeff took the blame upon himself. He expressed his love and appreciation for his father-in-law. He told him that as a private person and an independent individual he felt embarrassed to have a parent "check on him," even though he knew that his father-in-law's intentions were innocent. He went on to reassure his father-in-law that if ever he and Carla needed help or advice regarding any repairs, he would be the first one they'd call for help, being that he was so handy.

It took some time for the father-in-law to swallow his pride and accept Jeff's request. For a number of weeks, the relationship was somewhat strained. Carla talked to her father and reassured him of Jeff's love and respect for him, and eventually, he came to terms with the new situation.

By being truthful, respectful and direct, Jeff was able to achieve his goal without damaging the relationship with his father-in-law. Jeff was also wise to use an approach that would not put his father-in-law on the defensive, for the moment one feels accused is when communication most often breaks down. The idea is to have open lines of communication and taking responsibility, using "I" statements, such as "I feel..." or "I am..." as opposed to "You" statements, such as "You make me feel..." or "You are..."

Another notable point is that we must not forget that the notion of boundaries may differ between cultures. In this case, Jeff's father-in-law was an immigrant to the US and retained his culture's methods of showing interest by helping his daughter, whereas Jeff viewed his actions as unnecessary and overstepping boundaries.

Ruby

As I was preparing to leave a lecture I had given on the topic of in-laws, a woman approached me explaining, "In my culture the young couple moves in with the husband's parents, and that was horrible for me. My mother-in-law was in her domain and whatever I said was dismissed. We managed to have our own place eventually, with the hope that we would be more independent, but not wanting to leave my mother-in-law by herself when my father-in-law passed away, she moved in with us. She felt she was in her son's home and that allowed her to continue to run the show - she was still in charge. My husband had very little to say in the matter; respecting his mother was most important to him. If I had the guts to run away then I would have, but the culture did not allow that. I did vow, though, not to adhere to that custom when it came to our son. We live close to my son but my daughter-in-law is in charge in her home and I am merely a polite guest. You might say I learned my lesson the hard way."

We parted with a hug, but as she walked away, I tried to imagine the pain she must have endured for years, unable to be free of it due to cultural obligations.

Despite the great emotional impact on Ruby, caused by the experience with her husband's family, she did gain important insights which she is able to apply in her daily life. It is unfortunate that she endured this experience, but removing ourselves from

Bracha Loren, Psy.D, LMFT

the past and taking the positive lessons with us for the future, is an essential part of healing. The negative behavior inflicted upon Ruby allowed her to understand the different needs of others and as such, to treat her own daughter-in-law with care and respect.

Pauline and Morris

Pauline and Morris, an elderly couple, were patients of mine twenty years ago. They met in Europe after WWII, during which each had lost their families. They married and a year later became parents to a son, Harry, whom they considered their miracle. Eventually, the family of three made their way to the United States filled with dreams and hopes "for a new life." Their immediate focus was to find work so they could provide well for Harry. "He deserved a good life, to make up for the indescribable tragedies we suffered during the war," they told me.

The couple achieved their goal: Harry did very well in school, continued on to law school, and eventually established his own law firm. Harry met his future wife, Tanya, and together they seemed to have a nice relationship with Pauline and Morris. But once they were married, Harry would often tell his parents that Tanya did not feel completely accepted by them and thought they were "hovering over their son too much." Pauline and Morris felt that Tanya had no empathy for their "indescribable tragedy" during the war, nor was she interested in hearing about it.

During a family dinner, Pauline and Morris spoke of their unfortunate plight during the war, when suddenly Tanya announced, "I don't think this is conversation fit for a family dinner. I leave here depressed every time." Tanya's words were so offensive to Pauline

Bracha Loren, Psy.D, LMFT

and Morris that they decided they would only see Tanya on special occasions.

One day, Pauline met Katia, a young woman whom she thought would have been a far more suitable partner for her son than Tanya, and told Harry about Katia. At the next holiday gathering, Harry was surprised that his mother invited Katia to join. Pauline later revealed that she was secretly hoping Harry would fall for Katia and leave his wife.

At the only session Tanya and Harry accompanied Pauline and Morris to my office, Tanya said that during that dinner, Pauline continuously made "inappropriate comments that made my blood pressure rise." She suspected that Pauline was being sneaky in some way by having invited Katia for dinner. During the joint session, when Tanya asked her mother-in-law why she included Katia at the dinner, Pauline confessed that she thought Katia was more suitable for Harry. Tanya felt humiliated and was furious at Pauline's lack of boundaries. She and Harry left my office, refusing to see Pauline and Morris ever again.

Six years later, Pauline and Morris made an appointment to see me, seeking help in reuniting with their son. They had not spoken since that fateful day in my office. They expressed their concern about getting old, estranged from their son, and with no other family to speak of, they were very lonely. In therapy, they were able to come to terms with their son's life choices and their inappropriate interference. They said they wanted to include Harry and Tanya in family therapy, but the couple refused. The refusal was accompanied by a heartbreaking letter. In it, Harry poured his heart out to his parents to let them know how disappointed he was in them. He wrote that he could "take it if it had just been me," but he could never forgive them for humiliating Tanya. He told them that he and Tanya now had two children, but had no intention to introduce them to their grandchildren.

Pauline and Morris both passed away several years ago and Harry, conflicted, came to see me. His pain was obvious as he shared with me his disappointment and frustration with his parents. While he had come to terms with the reality of the situation, at the same time he felt great remorse and expressed feelings of guilt for not trying to reconcile with his parents while they were alive. Though Harry appreciated his parents wanting him to have a good life, he suffered from their lack of respect and consideration for his choice of wife. He said that he felt sorry for them and what they had experienced in life, but that was no excuse for their deeds. Pauline and Morris' wishes for Harry's happiness have come to fruition. Harry only wishes they could have shared in his happiness.

Thus ended the sad saga of an old couple who, by rejecting their daughter-in-law, lost their son in the process.

Nora

In some cultures the spouses are introduced to each other by their families and sometimes the marriage is arranged at birth. In the case of Nora, she still had not decided who her son's wife would be. He was still quite young when, during one of her sessions in my office, she described the place where the nuptials would take place. She knew the florist she would hire, the caterer, and the band that would play. I asked her if it was not premature to plan a wedding without a bride, who might have other ideas for her own wedding. She did not welcome my question. When I brought up the notion of a mother-in-law's boundaries, she dismissed that suggestion. "Boundaries?" She asked, "This is my only son. Any bride we choose for him should be happy to have him as a husband."

I have come to understand that each culture has its own expectations and customs, and this is not for anyone else to judge. However, what I do wish to comment on is that for there to be a harmonious relationship in this particular situation, Nora's future daughter-in-law must either be of the same cultural background as Nora's or at least understand the culture she is entering. On the other hand, if Nora's son marries a woman of a different culture or someone who does not adhere to the same rules as hers, there will be great conflict. It is best that Nora change her own expectations and prepare herself mentally that her son may marry a woman of his choice who is independent and makes her own rules. Nora's need to control the situation may end up being the biggest source of conflict in this future relationship.

Is It Never Too Late?

There is a phenomenon that I have noticed where parents-in-law, who do not accept the family newcomer, wisen up much too late, after their child has divorced their partner.

SANDRA AND ETTY

Sandra and Etty, two women in their late thirties, were married after a long courtship. According to Sandra, Etty's parents found it difficult to accept that their daughter was gay; consequently, it was very difficult for them to agree to the marriage. On top of that, they did not think Sandra was "good enough" for their daughter. At the end, they did attend the wedding but the relationship remained strained.

After one year of marriage, Sandra and Etty had a daughter, whom the grandparents were "absolutely crazy about." But there were so many disagreements between Sandra and her mother-in-law pertaining to how the child should be raised, that it caused considerable friction between Sandra and Etty. Sandra wished Etty's mother would "mind her own business" and Etty said that her mother had the right to express her wishes regarding her granddaughter. Sandra could no longer tolerate her mother-in-law's interference and judgment, and Etty could no longer tolerate having to defend her mother; eventually Sandra and Etty divorced.

After the separation, Sandra would occasionally bring her daughter to visit the grandparents. To Sandra's surprise, she and her ex-mother-in-law were more friendly during those visits than they had ever been while Sandra and Etty were together. What's more, when Etty became seriously involved with another woman, her mother expressed concern about this new woman to Sandra, as if they were old friends. Etty's mother went so far as to ask Sandra to "take Etty back."

"Why now?" Sandra would say bewildered and wry. Unfortunately, Sandra's ex-mother-in-law got to know and appreciate Sandra too late in the game. She had essentially meddled to the point of ruining the relationship between Sandra and Etty; yet, once Sandra was no longer a threat to her, she began to value Sandra as a person, and realized her error.

As I mentioned earlier, this is a phenomenon which I have encountered numerous times throughout my

Bracha Loren, Psy.D, LMFT

career. If one has the ability to analyze their own bias towards another individual and recognize the root of it, be it insecurity, closed mindedness, etc., only then will they be able to look forward and act constructively. We must identify the good in people and make those qualities our focus, rather than their inadequacies, for the former is the surest way to set up any relationship for success.

EVELYN AND KEVIN

After meeting in law school and graduating, Kevin and Evelyn were married and began looking for their first jobs. Kevin found work as a low-level employee at a local law firm, and Evelyn opened a private practice. Believing that Kevin lacked ambition, Evelyn's parents decided that they did not like Kevin and would make comments to Evelyn at any given opportunity, about Kevin being lazy. Kevin tried to form a relationship with his father-in-law, but Evelyn's father never regarded his son-in-law as an equal. Kevin expressed his pain about this perception to Evelyn. But as much as she would argue with her parents about their "rude behavior and remarks," it eventually "got to her" and she began criticizing Kevin to the point that he asked for a divorce. And so the two divorced, sharing custody of their two children.

Evelyn's family continued to invite Kevin to all family functions. "For the sake of the kids," Kevin said, he would go. During those gatherings, Evelyn's father would invite his former son-in-law to watch games on television, or have a drink in the back yard. The father-in-law had never before reached out in such a way and over time, the two men became quite friendly and found that they shared many common interests.

In my first sessions with Kevin, he described the evolution of his relationship with his ex-father-in-law. He expressed both great regret that they were not able to connect earlier, and joy that they were now on such wonderful terms. At the same time he was remorseful that his ex-wife had been so influenced by her father, and that this influence destroyed their marriage. Needless to say, Kevin had very mixed feelings about the present situation.

Sometimes the best lessons learned are through our own pain. At this point, while not being able to change the past, Kevin took the valuable lessons of acceptance and respect with him and was adamant that he would apply these principles with his own children.

Without realizing the effects of their words and actions, when in-laws neglect to make an effort to get to know their child's partner, they often fall victim to their own superficiality and this inadvertently often causes great damage to their child's relationship.

Attitude is Everything

A common thread that has been alluded to in the previously cited vignettes, is that if one experiences a not-so-perfect relationship, most likely the other party shares the discomfort. So, how does one resolve such conflict? In my experience, the only way for such resolution is that one party needs to take the initiative to approach the other. Generally, it is the more secure individual that will gather the courage to do so. The best approach is to reflect on one's own feelings regarding an event, rather than accusing the other party and making them responsible for those feelings. For example, stating, "In this situation I felt…" NOT, "You made/make me feel…" This practice has been discussed in previous pages, as it is very important to internalize this idea and be cognizant of it while communicating. Speaking in generalities and accusations will most likely not resolve the issue, but rather add fuel to it.

Another dynamic may be that only one party feels frustration and discomfort, unbeknownst to the other party. As a result, the behavior of the frustrated individual will most likely reflect these feelings. Although there is no conflict yet, this is the ideal time for the frustrated party to gently assert themselves, as seen in the case of Carla and Jeff (page 65), in order to prevent increased frustration. In any other situation, one may walk away, put the relationship on hold, or simply do nothing and continue the resentment. But what sets the in-law relationship apart from others, is that it is one that is "given," not "chosen;" it is presented to us as parents, as siblings, as wives, as husbands, or as children, and we must accept it.

As much as overall acceptance of the in-law relationship is essential to simply getting along, accepting our in-laws as individuals with unique personalities and idiosyncrasies is also essential to harmonious co-existence. We all have idiosyncrasies and we tend to tolerate them better in others when we recognize that we possess them as well. When they are different from ours, we may often find them irritating. While it may be a natural tendency to want to pounce, it would be wiser to step back and consider whether it is worth damaging a relationship based on behavior that may be out of another's control, as in the case of David and Reuben (page 47). We must accept others for who they are and not try to change them.

Wanda and Henry

Wanda and Henry come to mind to illustrate this. They are planning to get married as soon as they have the necessary funds for a down payment for a house. To increase their savings, they are living with Henry's parents. Wanda loves Henry's mother though she does find her behavior rather overbearing. "She does everything for him, even his laundry," she said. She and Henry have an understanding that when they are to move into their own place, he will take care of himself and not expect her to replace his mother. "For now, I am patiently living with her quirks - doing his laundry, needing to be involved in everything. I understand her not wanting to 'lose' her son. My mom was the same way with my brother. But once we get married, it will all change." Wanda never passes judgment and once Henry made the promise to take care of his affairs, she has not discussed the matter any further.

I am impressed by Wanda's decision to resolve her concerns with Henry directly and not bring it up with his mother. By doing so, she shows empathy and acceptance of her future mother-in-law. Further, if she confronts her about these habits, the relationship may be deeply damaged, and she does not think it is necessary to try to change her.

Angie and Guy

Angie and Guy have been married for eight years and are parents to three children. Quite often there are family gatherings; however, these gatherings always take place at their home, as Guy's parents never invite the family to their own home. When Angie has approached Guy, asking why this is the case, Guy states that his parents are very affectionate with the kids and love them, but "that's just who my parents are. They're funny like that."

At the beginning of the relationship, Angie took this as a personal affront. She could not understand why, if indeed Guy's parents loved them as he said, did they not welcome them into their home as Angie and Guy welcomed them. Initially, Angie and Guy argued over this point. Angie would feel frustrated and Guy would feel as if he needed to defend his parents. Angie came to see me after a particularly heated argument with Guy. Talking it through, she would say, "I know I can't change them and I wish I could." It took several sessions for Angie to realize that the only person she could control was herself and her attitude. We decided together that as an experiment, Angie should try for the next month to tell herself whenever frustrated, "This is who they are and it's not personal." After repeating this exercise several times, it has slowly become a new way of thinking for Angie and her frustration with both her in-laws, and as a result, with Guy, has greatly diminished. This is a wonderful example of how changing one's attitude can completely change a situation. It is a great reminder that because we cannot control others, change within ourselves is essential. Adjusting our thinking takes time and practice though and working hard at this is the only way to see positive results.

In the Bible

The Bible is a rich resource of practically every life situation and relational issue. Whether the relationships are between husbands and wives, parents and children, siblings, in-laws, and other family members, the Biblical events that take place provide a wealth of life lessons. The following Biblical accounts will exemplify the complexity of in-law relationships and will demonstrate the timelessness of the conflicts and successes we face today. To quote King Solomon, "There is nothing new under the sun" (The Book of Kohelet [Ecclesiastes] circa 450-200 BCE).

JACOB AND LABAN
(Genesis 29:26)

Traditionally, in Biblical times, the highest blessings were to be bestowed upon the first born son. The Bible tells of twin brothers Esau, the first born, and Jacob. Jacob, aided by his mother Rebecca, plotted and deceived his elderly father, whose eyes were too dim to see, by pretending to be Esau, with the intention of receiving the blessing reserved for his brother.

Once he was blessed by his father, fearing his brother's revenge, Jacob fled to the home of his mother's brother, Laban. There, he fell in love with his cousin Rachel, Laban's youngest daughter. In return for Rachel's hand in marriage, Jacob agreed to work seven years for his uncle. Not until after the wedding, when the couple awoke the following morning, did Jacob realize that the woman next to him was not Rachel but her older sister Leah. Laban, his uncle-turned-father-in-law, had deceived him!

Laban excused his deception, saying, "It is not the practice of our place to marry off the younger before the older." Laban again promised to give Rachel's hand in marriage to Jacob if he worked for him seven more years. Jacob swallowed his pride and with the hope that this time his uncle would honor his promise, agreed to work for his uncle seven more years, at the end of which he indeed married his beloved Rachel.

In today's Western world, it is hard to imagine a son-in-law who would continue to endure such humiliation and deceit. But in those days, cultural standards were different. Even though deceit was not new to Jacob, that would not soften his distrust towards his father-in-law. We tend to empathize with Jacob as he contained his resentment and made what seemed to him, a worthwhile sacrifice. It must have been disheartening to live with a father-in-law whose each promise was suspicious. He knew that Laban was not to be trusted, and after a total of twenty years of working for him, Jacob was ready to return to his home.

Knowing the dishonest nature of his father-in-law, he left with his wives, children, and rightfully gained livestock, without letting Laban know, lest he try to take away his property. Ten days later, Laban caught up with Jacob and eventually the two men were able to make peace and each went on his way.

One can only speculate how Jacob was able to move past Laban's deceit. For twenty years he lived under the rule of his distrustful father-in-law. Perhaps over the years he developed insight into his own character flaw, for he himself had committed a great transgression against his twin brother and father. This recognition may have enabled him to live under those conditions, as we tend to tolerate the flaws in others more easily when we recognize them in ourselves.

TAMAR AND JUDAH
(Genesis 38:6-28)

According to the custom of the day, if a husband dies childless, his brother would marry the widow and have a child with her; this child will carry the deceased husband's name.

Judah had three sons. The oldest was married to Tamar, but before they could have children, "… the Lord took his life." As Tamar was now a widow, Judah instructed his next oldest son to, "Join with your brother's wife and do your duty by her as a brother-in-law, and provide offspring for your brother." But the second son, "knowing that the seed would not count as his, let it go to waste whenever he joined with his brother's wife." For that, the Lord took his life as well.

At this point, Judah instructed his daughter-in-law, "Stay as a widow in your father's house until my third son grows up." Wishing to obey her father-in-law, Tamar returned to her family home. But Judah, fearing that his third and youngest son may share his brothers' fate, decided to save his son's life by not giving him as a husband to Tamar; thus going back on his promise to her.

When Tamar discovered that Judah's third son had grown up, "yet she had not been given to him as wife," it became clear to her that her father-in-law had no intention of fulfilling his promise to her. Tamar was determined to have a child and decided to design her

Bracha Loren, Psy.D, LMFT

own fate. So, when Judah was preparing to come to her town, Tamar "took off her widow's garb, covered her face with a veil..." She sat down at the entrance to her town, and upon Judah's arrival he "took her for a harlot." Not realizing her identity, he slept with her, and as payment for her service, he promised to send her a sheep. But Tamar had a plan and still asked for his "seal and cord, and the staff which you carry" as collateral. Judah agreed and Tamar went away. When Judah's servant came to deliver the promised sheep to Tamar, she was gone.

Three months later, when Judah was told, "Your daughter-in-law, Tamar… is with child by harlotry," he exclaimed, "Bring her out and let her be burned." As Tamar was brought out, she sent a message to Judah, along with the seal and cord, and staff, saying, "I am with child by the man to whom these belong." Recognizing his belongings, Judah said, "She is more in the right than I, inasmuch as I did not give her to my son."

As it turned out, Tamar achieved her goal. She was blessed to have twins who would carry her husband's name and Judah admitted his guilt, taking full responsibility when he could have denied it. While this situation would be considered outlandish if it happened today, there are several lessons to be learned that can be applied in modern times. Yes, Tamar was deceitful but it was for self-preservation, not self-serving. She was not trying to hurt her father-in-law, as she treated him respectfully, never embarrassing him publicly, never revealing the secret, even to save herself; rather, she was protecting herself while remaining loyal to her father-in-law. Conversely, yes, Judah was conniving, but he too was acting in the name of self-preservation. He was protecting his youngest son from the possibility of death, not specifically intending to hurt Tamar.

As in many instances, we want to judge who is right and who is wrong but it is often difficult to live in black and white terms. It is essential to see the entire story and the motivation of the participants before we may pass judgment.

Joseph and Potifar's Wife
(Genesis 39:7-21, 41:45)

In a sequence of tragic events, Joseph ended up as a personal attendant in the household of Potifar, the chief steward of Pharaoh. After an unsuccessful attempt to seduce Joseph, Potifar's wife proceeds to accuse him of seducing her. As a result, Joseph is put in an Egyptian jail. Eventually, Joseph marries Potifar's daughter, Osnat, the daughter of the very woman who had accused him of sexual harassment.

We can only speculate what sort of mother-in-law Potifar's wife must have been, after having fabricated such an egregious crime. From the onset of the marriage, the relationship between Joseph and his mother-in-law would appear to have been doomed. Yet, this does not seem to have prevented Joseph and Osnat from raising two sons who flourished and eventually were counted among the tribes of Israel. The chaotic in-law relationship does not appear to have negatively impacted Joseph and Osnat and their children.

I often reflect on this story when I meet a couple whose mother-in-law or father-in-law has behaved in a way that is unforgivable, as hope for the couple to persevere and live a fulfilling and happy life together. Couples can achieve great success when they are a strong unit even when they must withstand complex outside interferences.

JETHRO AND MOSES
(Exodus 38:17-24)

We are told that Moses was a great servant of God. He led his people from slavery to freedom, and while in the desert, he was their spiritual leader and judge: "...Moses sat as magistrate among the people while the people stood about Moses from morning until evening."

Jethro, Moses' Midianite father-in-law, seeing that his son-in-law was the only spiritual guide and judge of his people, recognized the toll that those tasks took on Moses, both emotionally and physically. Out of concern for his son-in-law, Jethro shared his observation with Moses and offered some valuable managerial advice: "The thing you are doing is not right. You will surely wear yourself out, and these people as well." He suggested that Moses assign "capable men who fear God, trustworthy men who will hate ill-gotten gain... as chiefs...let them judge the people at all times. Have them bring every major dispute to you...make it easier for you by letting them share the burden with you... You will be able to bear up; and all these people too will go home unwearied."

It may appear that Jethro, by taking the liberty of offering his son-in-law unsolicited advice, may have overstepped his boundaries. But Moses saw it differently. He knew the advice came from a good place, out of regard and care for him. As a result, he offered no dispute but rather, respecting his father-in-law's wisdom, accepted his advice: "Moses heeded his father-in-law and did just as he had said."

These two men, of different origins and cultural backgrounds, did not allow those differences to affect their relationship. They knew each other as human beings. Thanks to the mutual respect and trust that existed between them, and thanks to Moses' open mindedness, no conflict was created throughout this scenario.

Unsolicited advice may be interpreted as either helpful or as criticism, depending on the relationships between individuals. With many of my patients, I have found that the existing relationship between the in-laws will dictate how advice is received. Most often, in a trusting and open relationship, such advice will be looked at as constructive, hence it is welcome. If the relationship is fragile, any comment may bring about defensiveness and hurt feelings, because the advice might be taken as criticism. When one is about to give unsolicited advice, it is wise to pause and consider whether the relationship is strong enough to withstand misinterpretation.

RUTH AND NAOMI
(Ruth 1:16-17)

In the Book of Ruth, we are told of Naomi, who lost her husband and then her two married sons. Despite her immense losses, this generous and unselfish "older widow" was more concerned with the welfare of the two "younger widows," her daughters-in-law, than her own pain and suffering.

Though she risked being left alone, Naomi advised her daughters-in-law to return to their mothers' homes and create new lives for themselves. One of them, Orpah, followed Naomi's advice, and after an emotional parting from her mother-in-law, returned to her family home. Naomi's other daughter-in-law, Ruth, chose to stay with Naomi, famously saying, "Don't urge me to leave you or to turn back from you. Where you go I will go and where you stay I will stay... if even death separates you and me."

Clearly, Naomi was a loving, empathetic mother-in-law all along. Ruth's decision to stay with her demonstrates the strong and close relationship the two women shared, and explains the loyalty that Ruth felt towards her.

What is so fascinating about the relationship between Naomi and Ruth is that Naomi and Ruth came from completely different cultures. Naomi was Jewish and Ruth was Moabite. Yet, despite this significant difference, their love for each other transcended culture and religion.

Bracha Loren, Psy.D, LMFT

For Grandparents

***

Most parents look forward to their children building their own families, and future grandchildren are an integral part of that vision. The dual role of grandparent/in-law requires a fine balance. Grandparents may feel that they have "been there, done that" and now know it all, but they do not. Repeatedly I hear comments from frustrated daughters-in-law that their mothers-in-law are too influential in how the grandchildren should be raised, contradicting the mothers' ideas. This will often lead to unnecessary arguments. As much as they love their grandchildren, grandparents need to remember that their grandchildren have their own parents, and they, too, have the children's best interest at heart, and the final say in their offspring's' affairs.

Once, when I babysat for a few days for my son and his wife while they were out of town, my grandchildren and I were invited to join another family for a great outing that the kids would have surely enjoyed.

However, my daughter-in-law had made other plans for the kids. Even though I could have easily cancelled those plans and accepted the new invitation, which was tempting, I needed to remind myself that as the grandmother, I had no authority to make any changes to their mother's plans without her agreement. I had to respect my daughter-in-law's wishes by following the plans that she had set up for her children.

This principle applies to discipline as well. That responsibility is left for the parents only, unless asked by the parents to do so. Grandparents, the link in the chain, are there to love, encourage, and accept the grandchildren unconditionally. That is what the young ones will remember.

The most common criticism I hear from sons and daughters-in-law towards the grandparents is regarding food, or more often, sweets, given to the grandchildren. In fact, I hear this complaint on a regular basis. While it may sound trivial to a grandparent, innocently disregarding the wishes of the parents on this subject feels dismissive and disrespectful. I propose that grandparents ask the parents if they may offer the pancakes, candy, chocolate, etc. before offering it to the grandchildren and accepting, without judgment, the parents' wishes. It is a simple gesture that will speak volumes. Grandparents have to recognize and be mindful of their boundaries; crossing them may not be appreciated and may interrupt the harmony of their grown child's household. Harmony among all in-laws and all sets of grandparents will make the relationships with the grandchildren so much more enjoyable and fulfilling.

Len

Before I married Len, I had the occasion to briefly meet his mother. Sadly, she was on her death bed and could hardly talk. It was impossible to hold a full conversation so instead, I sang to her. Knowing the end was near, she smiled at me, and in her faint voice said, "If he does not listen to you, hit him over the head." That was a very endearing show of acceptance; it felt delightful. No doubt she would have been a wonderful mother-in-law had she lived longer.

Len was a child psychiatrist in partial retirement when we married. I had four children from my first marriage. Now, with a new set of responsibilities, Len decided to continue working, "to keep the children in the lifestyle they were used to," as he put it. He was happy to work full-time again, and took care of my kids with love, referring to them as "our children."

My mother, having endured difficulty with her in-laws, did not prove to be the welcoming mother-in-law one would have expected her to become, which took me by surprise. Of course, we lived an ocean apart, so she had no chance to meet Len and get to know him, no opportunity to approve or disapprove of him. As far as she was concerned, my ex-husband had not been dismissed by her as her son-in-law; she was reluctant to accept a new one. And when she learned that Len was thirteen years my senior and nearing retirement, she was particularly unhappy. "How will the two of you support the four children?" she would ask.

I never shared my conversations with my mother with Len. I did not want to hurt him and I did not want him to develop negative feelings toward her. I was sure that once she met him she would love him, like everyone else who had ever known him.

At last, she did meet Len. Being amidst our family, she realized what he meant to the children and me. My mother grew to love him and expressed regret for her initial doubts. That was when I realized how important it had been for me to keep my conversations with her private. Too many individuals prematurely share such information with their partners, instilling unnecessary negative feelings in them and creating conflicts that are not easy to repair.

My mother was a significant influence throughout my life, in every kind of relationship. She generously shared her experiences with me, encouraging me to learn from them. If she told me chocolate was sweet, I am sure I would have never tasted it to confirm; that is the extent of the trust I had in her. One of the most important pieces of advice she gave to me was that approaching any challenge to be resolved will require setting emotions aside and avoiding reactivity. Hence, my disappointment when she initially met Len and I found myself having to remind her of her words.

Unlike my mother, when my father learned of Len's commitment to my children and me, he immediately admired, appreciated, accepted and loved him unconditionally.

Len loved my parents before he even met them, declaring that by marrying me he was marrying my whole family, "In-laws and all." This is an important notion that must be remembered: Marrying into a family, practically speaking, means marrying the entire family.

While we all want to have our own experiences and learn on our own, learning from others has a great benefit. If we look at the improved relationship as an investment, it will prove to be the most profitable one you have made.

True, we cannot argue the fact that there is no manual for a mutually satisfying in-law relationship, or any other relationship for that matter. There are some ingredients, though, that when applied, will help create a successful recipe, that will be pleasing to the palette. How much to add or reduce will depend on the individuals involved, and the circumstances. There is no one formula suitable for all.

A reminder to the "incoming" member into the family:

These are the parents of your beloved. They raised him/her; recognize their influence on who your partner is.

A reminder to parents: This is your child's chosen partner; by accepting and respecting the new comer, you show respect to your own child.

Bracha Loren, Psy.D, LMFT

Ingredients for a Fruitful In-Law Relationship

1 *dash* Kindness

2 *tsps* Sensitivity to Differences

3 *cups* Patience

4 *liters* Empathy

5 *Tbsps* Truthfulness

6 *ounces* Trust

7 *sprinkles* Generosity

8 *pints* Forgiveness

9 *gallons* Respect of Differences

10 *tsps* Being Non-Judgmental

11 *cups* Acceptance

12 *Tbsps* Refraining from Criticism

13 *dashes* Minding Boundaries

14 *handfuls* Getting to Know the Person

15 *ounces* Humility

End Note

The people who were at my side during this process, and to whom I owe my gratitude and thanks are my daughter Dr. Talia Schwartz, my daughter-in-law Dr. Daphna Barak, Amanda Sthers, Dr. Guy Maruani, Guy Babagilo, Angie Paventy, and Tammy Thompson.

My thanks are hitherto expressed also to the individuals in the above vignettes, who allowed me to share their "stories," and whose names have been altered in order to preserve their privacy and identities.

—B. L.